The entrepreneur's guide to success

The Definitive Roadmap to Navigating the Entrepreneurial Journey to Success

By

Arnold c Hoffman

Chapter 8. Adapting to Industry Trends and Disruptions.

- Conclusion

Introduction

Welcome to the Entrepreneur's Guide to Success, a comprehensive roadmap for aspiring and established entrepreneurs navigating the dynamic landscape of business ownership. In this guide, we embark on an enlightening journey that unveils the fundamental principles, strategies, and indispensable tools crucial for achieving entrepreneurial success in today's competitive world. Whether you're a visionary innovator venturing into uncharted territory or a seasoned entrepreneur seeking to refine your strategies, this guide offers invaluable insights, actionable advice, and proven methodologies to help you chart a course toward achieving your entrepreneurial aspirations. Join us as we explore the essential elements that pave the way for entrepreneurial triumph and guide you through the intricacies of building a thriving enterprise.

The information contained in this book is for general informational purposes only. While every effort has been made to ensure the accuracy, completeness, and reliability of the information presented, the author does not assume any responsibility for any errors, inaccuracies, omissions, or outcomes resulting from the use of this information. The content within this book is not intended to serve as professional advice or replace consultation with qualified professionals in specific fields. Readers are advised to use their discretion and seek appropriate guidance or professional assistance as needed in relation to any specific matter. The author and publisher shall have no liability or responsibility to any person or entity regarding any loss or damage incurred, directly or indirectly, from the information contained in this book. The views and opinions expressed herein are those of the author and do not necessarily reflect the views of the publisher. Any resemblance to actual persons, living or dead, or actual events is purely coincidental. All rights reserved. No part of this publication may be reproduced, stored in a retrieval system, or transmitted in any form or by any means, electronic, mechanical, photocopying, recording, or otherwise, without prior written permission from the author or publisher.

Chapter 1
Developing a Growth Mindset.

Developing a growth mindset is a transformative journey that involves cultivating a mindset focused on continuous learning, resilience, and embracing challenges as opportunities for growth. Here are steps to foster a growth mindset:

1. Embrace Challenges: View challenges as opportunities for learning and development rather than obstacles. Embrace them with a positive attitude, seeing them as a chance to expand your abilities.

2. Value Effort and Persistence:
Understand that effort and persistence are essential components of success. Embrace the process of learning and improvement, even if faced with setbacks or failures.

3. Learn from Criticism: Be open to feedback and constructive criticism. Use feedback as a tool for growth, recognizing that it provides insights and opportunities for improvement.

4. Celebrate Growth and Effort:
Acknowledge and celebrate your progress, focusing on the efforts and strategies that lead to improvement, rather than solely on immediate outcomes.

5. Adopt a "Yet" Mentality: Replace fixed thoughts like "I can't do this" with a growth-oriented mindset by adding "yet." For instance, "I can't do this yet, but I'm working on it."

6. Cultivate Curiosity and Learning: Foster a curiosity-driven approach to learning. Explore new ideas, seek out knowledge, and continuously challenge yourself to expand your skill set and understanding.

7. Redefine Failures as Learning Opportunities: View failures as stepping stones toward growth and learning. Analyze what went wrong, learn from the experience, and adapt your approach for future endeavors.

8. Surround Yourself with Growth-Oriented Individuals: Engage with people who have a growth mindset. Their attitudes and perspectives can influence your own mindset and support your growth journey.

9. Set Growth-Oriented Goals: Set goals that focus on continuous improvement rather than fixed achievements. Break these goals into smaller, achievable steps that encourage learning and development.

10. Practice Self-Compassion: Be kind to yourself when facing challenges or setbacks. Understand that setbacks are a natural part of the learning process, and self-compassion fosters resilience.

By consistently applying these principles and approaches, individuals can gradually develop and nurture a growth mindset, enabling them to adapt, learn, and flourish in various aspects of life and work.

Chapter 2
Identifying and Evaluating Business Opportunities.

Identifying and evaluating business opportunities is a critical process that involves thorough analysis and strategic thinking. Here's a guide on how to approach this:

1. Market Research: Conduct comprehensive market research to identify potential opportunities. Analyze market trends, customer needs, competitor landscape, and emerging industries to uncover gaps or areas with untapped potential.

2. Assess Your Skills and Interests: Consider your strengths, skills, and interests. Look for opportunities that align with your expertise and passions, as this can increase your chances of success and satisfaction.

3. Problem-Solving Approach: Identify problems or pain points in the market and explore opportunities to offer solutions. Businesses that address pressing needs tend to have higher chances of success.

4. SWOT Analysis: Conduct a SWOT (Strengths, Weaknesses, Opportunities, Threats) analysis to assess the feasibility and potential risks associated with the identified opportunities. Evaluate internal strengths and weaknesses along with external opportunities and threats.

5. Validate Demand: Validate the demand for your proposed product or service. Consider conducting surveys, interviews, or creating prototypes to gather feedback from potential customers.

6. Financial Viability: Assess the financial feasibility of the opportunity. Estimate startup costs, potential revenue, and profitability. Evaluate whether the opportunity aligns with your budget and financial goals.

7. Scalability and Growth Potential: Consider the scalability and growth potential of the opportunity. Evaluate if it can grow sustainably over time and adapt to changing market conditions.

8. Legal and Regulatory Considerations: Understand the legal and regulatory requirements associated with the business opportunity. Ensure compliance with laws, permits, and industry regulations.

9. Assess Risks: Identify potential risks and challenges associated with the opportunity. Develop contingency plans or strategies to mitigate these risks.

10. Competitive Analysis: Analyze the competitive landscape. Identify direct and indirect competitors, their strengths, weaknesses, and market positioning. Determine how your offering can differentiate itself.

11. Create a Business Plan: Develop a comprehensive business plan that outlines your strategy, target market, marketing plan, operational details, financial projections, and growth strategies.

12. Continuous Evaluation and Adaptation: Business opportunities evolve, so continuously evaluate and adapt your strategies based on market feedback, changing trends, and customer needs.

All these are the steps that conduct a thorough evaluation, entrepreneurs can identify and assess business opportunities effectively, increasing the likelihood of success when pursuing new ventures.

Chapter 3
Building a Strong Business Plan

Creating a strong business plan is essential for guiding your business's growth and securing funding. Here's a step-by-step guide to building a comprehensive business plan:

1. Executive Summary: Summarize the key elements of your business plan, including your business idea, goals, target market, unique value proposition, and financial projections. This section should provide a snapshot of your entire plan.

2. Business Description: Provide an overview of your business. Describe your business concept, mission, vision, and the problem your product/service solves. Explain the industry you operate in and the market needs you aim to address.

3. Market Analysis: Conduct a detailed analysis of your target market, including its size, demographics, trends, and growth potential. Identify your competitors and analyze their strengths, weaknesses, and market positioning.

4. Products or Services: Describe your products or services in detail. Explain their features, benefits, and how they meet the needs of your target market. Highlight any unique selling propositions or competitive advantages.

5. Marketing and Sales Strategy: Outline your marketing and sales approach. Define your target audience, distribution channels, pricing strategy, promotional tactics, and sales forecast. Explain how you plan to acquire and retain customers.

6. Operational Plan: Describe the operational aspects of your business. Detail your production process, suppliers, logistics, technology requirements, facilities, and any legal or regulatory considerations.

7. Management and Organization:
Outline the organizational structure of your business. Introduce key team members, their roles, expertise, and responsibilities. Highlight their relevant experience and qualifications.

8. Financial Projections: Present detailed financial forecasts, including income statements, cash flow projections, and balance sheets. Include sales forecasts, expense estimates, break-even analysis, and funding requirements.

9. Funding Request (if applicable): If seeking funding, specify the amount you need, the purpose of funds, and how you plan to use them. Clearly outline the return on investment for potential investors or lenders.

10. Appendix: Include supplementary information, such as resumes of key team members, market research data, legal documents, or additional financial information.

11. Review and Refinement: Regularly review and refine your business plan. Update it as your business evolves, market conditions change, or new opportunities arise.

A well-crafted business plan serves as a roadmap, helping you make informed decisions, attract investors or lenders, and steer your business toward success. Tailor your plan to your specific business needs and audience, ensuring it communicates a clear and compelling vision for your venture.

Chapter 4
Effective Marketing and Branding Strategies.

Effective marketing and branding strategies are crucial for businesses to build awareness, engage customers, and differentiate themselves in the market. Here are some key strategies:

1. Define Your Brand Identity: Clearly define your brand's identity, including its values, mission, and unique selling proposition (USP). Ensure consistency in messaging and visual elements across all channels.

2. Know Your Audience: Understand your target audience deeply. Create detailed buyer personas to identify their needs, preferences, behaviors, and pain points. Tailor your marketing efforts to resonate with your audience.

3. Content Marketing: Develop valuable and relevant content that educates, entertains, or solves problems for your audience. Use a mix of formats like blog posts, videos, infographics, and podcasts to engage your audience.

4. Social Media Engagement: Leverage social media platforms to connect with your audience. Create engaging content, interact with followers, run targeted ads, and use analytics to optimize your social media strategy.

5. Search Engine Optimization (SEO): Optimize your website and content for search engines. Focus on relevant keywords, high-quality content, user experience, and link building to improve your visibility in search results.

6. Email Marketing: Build and nurture relationships with your audience through email campaigns. Personalize content, segment your audience, and provide valuable information, promotions, or updates.

7. Influencer Marketing: Collaborate with influencers or industry experts who resonate with your audience. Their endorsement can help expand your reach and credibility within your niche.

8. Customer Experience: Focus on delivering exceptional customer experiences. Provide outstanding service, listen to customer feedback, and address concerns promptly to build brand loyalty and positive word-of-mouth.

9. Branding Consistency: Ensure consistency in branding across all touchpoints, including your website, social media, packaging, customer service, and advertising. A cohesive brand identity reinforces brand recognition and trust.

10. Partnerships and Collaborations: Explore partnerships or collaborations with other brands or organizations that align with your values or target audience. Joint initiatives can widen your reach and create new opportunities.

11. Measure and Analyze Results: Use analytics and key performance indicators (KPIs) to track the performance of your marketing efforts. Analyze data to understand what strategies are working and make data-driven decisions.

12. Adapt and Evolve: Continuously adapt your marketing strategies based on market trends, consumer behavior, and feedback. Stay agile and be ready to adjust strategies to remain relevant and competitive.

Implementing these marketing and branding strategies, while consistently refining and adapting them, can help businesses effectively reach their target audience, build brand awareness, and foster long-term relationships with customers.

Chapter 5
Navigating Financing Options.

Navigating financing options is crucial for businesses seeking capital to start, operate, or expand. Here are various financing options available:

1. Self-Funding (Bootstrapping): Use personal savings, assets, or credit cards to fund your business. This method gives you full control but involves personal financial risk.

2. Friends and Family: Seek loans or investments from friends and family members who believe in your business idea.

Clearly outline terms and agreements to avoid misunderstandings.

3. Traditional Bank Loans: Apply for small business loans from banks or credit unions. These loans typically require collateral and a good credit history but offer lower interest rates compared to alternative options.

4. Small Business Administration (SBA) Loans: SBA offers various loan programs with favorable terms for small businesses, including microloans, 7(a) loans, and CDC/504 loans. They are partially guaranteed by the SBA, making them more accessible to qualifying businesses.

5. Venture Capital (VC) and Angel Investors: Venture capitalists and angel investors provide capital in exchange for equity or ownership stakes in the company. They often invest in high-growth potential startups but may require a significant share of the business.

6. Crowdfunding: Raise funds from a large number of individuals through crowdfunding platforms like Kickstarter, Indiegogo, or GoFundMe. Offer rewards, pre-sales, or equity in exchange for contributions.

7. Grants and Competitions: Look for grants, business competitions, or government programs offering funding to support specific industries, innovation, or social initiatives. These often do not require repayment but have specific eligibility criteria.

8. Business Incubators and Accelerators: Join business incubator or accelerator programs that offer funding, mentorship, and resources in exchange for equity or a percentage of future revenue.

9. Alternative Financing Options: Explore alternative financing methods such as equipment financing, invoice financing, merchant cash advances, or revenue-based financing, depending on your business needs.

10. Corporate Partnerships or Strategic Alliances: Collaborate with larger companies or industry partners that may provide funding, resources, or investments in exchange for joint initiatives or strategic alliances.

When navigating financing options, consider factors such as the amount of capital required, repayment terms, interest rates, equity stakes, eligibility criteria, and the impact on your business's long-term goals. Evaluate each option carefully to choose the one that best suits your business needs and financial situation. Consulting with financial advisors or business experts can also provide valuable guidance in choosing the right financing avenue.

Chapter 6
Mastering Time and Productivity Management.

Mastering time and productivity management is essential for maximizing efficiency and achieving goals. Here are strategies to improve time management and productivity:

1. Set Clear Goals: Define specific, measurable, achievable, relevant, and time-bound (SMART) goals. Having clear objectives helps prioritize tasks and stay focused.

2. Prioritize Tasks: Use techniques like Eisenhower's Urgent/Important Matrix or the ABCDE method to prioritize tasks based on their importance and urgency. Focus on high-priority tasks first.

3. Create a Schedule: Develop a daily or weekly schedule that allocates time for various tasks, including work, breaks, meetings, and personal activities. Stick to the schedule as much as possible.

4. Time Blocking: Allocate specific blocks of time for dedicated tasks or activities. Avoid multitasking and focus on one task during each time block to improve concentration and productivity.

5. Use To-Do Lists: Create to-do lists to organize tasks and track progress. Break down large tasks into smaller, manageable steps. Check off completed tasks for a sense of accomplishment.

6. Minimize Distractions: Identify and minimize distractions in your environment. Turn off notifications, designate specific time slots for checking emails or social media, and create a conducive workspace.

7. Set Deadlines and Milestones: Set deadlines for tasks and projects to maintain momentum and accountability. Break larger projects into smaller milestones to track progress effectively.

8. Utilize Time Management Tools: Use productivity tools and apps such as calendars, task managers, project management software, or time-tracking apps to organize tasks and enhance efficiency.

9. Delegate Tasks: Delegate tasks that others can handle effectively, allowing you to focus on higher-priority responsibilities. Trust your team and empower them to take on specific tasks.

10. Practice Time Batching: Group similar tasks together to streamline workflow. For instance, batch email responses, meetings, or creative work during specific time blocks.

11. Take Breaks and Rest: Incorporate regular breaks into your schedule to recharge. Breaks can boost productivity, creativity, and overall well-being.

12. Reflect and Review: Regularly review your productivity strategies and assess what works best for you. Adjust and refine your approach based on your observations and feedback.

Adopting these time management and productivity strategies requires commitment and consistent practice. Experiment with different techniques to find the methods that suit your work style and help you achieve optimal productivity.

Chapter 7
Developing Leadership and Team-building Skills.

Developing leadership and team-building skills is crucial for fostering a cohesive and high-performing team. Here are strategies to enhance these skills:

1. Lead by Example: Demonstrate integrity, professionalism, and a strong work ethic. Your actions set the tone for your team members to follow.

2. Effective Communication: Hone your communication skills. Be clear, open, and empathetic when communicating with team members. Actively listen and encourage open dialogue.

3. Set Clear Expectations: Clearly communicate goals, expectations, and roles within the team. Ensure that everyone understands their responsibilities and how their work contributes to the team's objectives.

4. Delegate and Empower: Delegate tasks and responsibilities to team members, giving them autonomy and opportunities for growth. Trust their capabilities and provide support when needed.

5. Encourage Collaboration: Foster a collaborative environment where team members can share ideas, collaborate on projects, and leverage each other's strengths. Encourage brainstorming sessions and diverse perspectives.

6. Provide Feedback: Offer constructive feedback regularly. Acknowledge achievements and address areas for improvement. Create a culture that values continuous learning and development.

7. Develop Emotional Intelligence: Understand and manage your emotions effectively. Empathize with team members' feelings and perspectives. Emotional intelligence helps build stronger relationships and resolves conflicts.

8. Promote Team Bonding: Organize team-building activities or events that promote camaraderie, trust, and a sense of belonging among team members. This helps improve morale and collaboration.

9. Conflict Resolution: Develop skills in resolving conflicts diplomatically and constructively. Address conflicts promptly and encourage open discussions to find mutually agreeable solutions.

10. Lead with Vision: Articulate a compelling vision for the team. Inspire and motivate team members by aligning their efforts with a shared vision and goals.

11. Continuous Learning: Invest in your own professional development. Attend leadership workshops, courses, or read books on leadership to enhance your skills and stay updated with industry trends.

12. Celebrate Achievements: Acknowledge and celebrate team achievements, milestones, and successes. Recognizing and rewarding accomplishments boosts morale and motivates team members.

13. Adaptability and Flexibility: Be adaptable to change and demonstrate flexibility in leadership. Embrace new ideas, adapt to evolving situations, and encourage innovation within the team.

Consistently practicing and honing these leadership and team-building skills can significantly contribute to creating a positive work environment, fostering collaboration, and achieving collective goals within a team. Leadership is an ongoing journey of learning and growth.

Chapter 8
Adapting to Industry Trends and Disruptions.

Adapting to industry trends and disruptions is crucial for businesses to remain competitive and thrive in a rapidly changing landscape. Here are strategies to navigate industry shifts effectively:

1. Stay Informed: Continuously monitor industry trends, technological advancements, and market changes. Stay updated through industry publications, networking, attending conferences, and following thought leaders.

2. Flexibility and Agility: Foster a culture of adaptability within your organization. Be open to change and encourage innovation. Create processes that allow for quick adjustments to changing circumstances.

3. Customer-Centric Approach: Focus on understanding customer needs and preferences. Adapt your products, services, and strategies based on evolving customer demands.

4. Embrace Technology: Embrace emerging technologies relevant to your industry. Explore how innovations like AI, automation, blockchain, or data analytics can improve efficiency, enhance products, or create new opportunities.

5. Collaboration and Partnerships:
Collaborate with industry peers, startups, or tech companies to leverage expertise, share resources, and stay ahead of industry disruptions. Strategic alliances can drive innovation.

6. Invest in R&D:
Allocate resources to research and development to innovate and stay ahead of market changes. Experiment with new ideas, products, or business models to adapt to emerging trends.

7. Adaptive Leadership: Leadership should promote and drive adaptation to change. Encourage a culture of learning, experimentation, and risk-taking within the organization.

8. Anticipate Future Trends: Predict future trends by analyzing data, consumer behavior, and market insights. Anticipating changes early allows for proactive adjustments rather than reactive measures.

9. Reskill and Upskill Employees: Invest in continuous learning and skill development for your workforce. Ensure that employees have the necessary skills to adapt to new technologies and changing roles.

10. Risk Management: Assess and mitigate risks associated with industry disruptions. Have contingency plans in place to minimize potential negative impacts on the business.

11. Customer Feedback and Iteration: Regularly collect and analyze customer feedback. Use this information to iterate and improve products, services, or processes in line with evolving market needs.

12. Regulatory and Compliance Awareness: Stay updated on regulatory changes that could impact your industry. Ensure compliance while remaining agile enough to adapt to new regulations.

Adapting to industry trends and disruptions requires proactive planning, strategic foresight, and a willingness to embrace change. By staying agile, innovative, and customer-focused, businesses can position themselves to not only survive but thrive in evolving market conditions.

Conclusion

In the intricate world of entrepreneurship, success is not merely a destination but a journey paved with resilience, innovation, and unwavering determination. This guide serves as a compass, offering invaluable insights, strategies, and wisdom to navigate the dynamic terrain of business ownership. It encapsulates the essence of strategic thinking, adaptability, and the relentless pursuit of excellence that defines the entrepreneurial spirit. Yet, beyond the strategies outlined lies a fundamental truth: true success stems from a passion-driven commitment to continuous learning, embracing failures as stepping stones, and daring to dream beyond conventional boundaries. Armed with this guide, aspiring and seasoned entrepreneurs alike embark on a transformative quest, not just to achieve success, but to carve a legacy fueled by innovation, purpose, and an unwavering entrepreneurial spirit.

www.ingramcontent.com/pod-product-compliance
Lightning Source LLC
Chambersburg PA
CBHW062257290526
45794CB00006B/2597